A **WORD** IN THE HAND
BOOK 2

Written by
Jane L. Kitterman
and
S. Harold Collins

Illustrated by
Kathy Kifer

A Breath of Fresh Air
GarlicPress

Published by
Garlic Press
100 Hillview Lane #2
Eugene, OR 97401

Reorder No. GP-042.

Preface

A WORD IN THE HAND, BOOK 2 is a response to its predecessor, A WORD IN THE HAND: *An Introduction to Sign Language.* With that book, we established a format to present, practice, and review basic Signed English.

A WORD IN THE HAND, BOOK 2 picks up the basics acquired from Book 1 to expand signing vocabulary and signing facility while simultaneously reinforcing the patterns of Standard English. This second book is well suited for the structured classroom from middle grades through college. It is also well suited for the community setting where children, young adults, and adults desire to advance signing skills.

Teaching Format

The 10 lessons in Book 2 follow a teaching procedure which includes: a skill game, a review of previous material, an introduction to new vocabulary, practice, and an assignment. A certain degree of flexibilty exists in each procedural step, allowing the instructor to focus, slow, or accelerate as needs pertain to those being taught.

Although all vocabulary is accompanied by an illustration, demonstration is imperative to present a sign which can then be reinforced by the illustration. Demonstrate first. Use the illustration for reference and recall. Annotate the pictures if necessary.

Once again, please remember that signs can vary significantly owing to local or regional preferences. We have illustrated signs to satisfy a most common usage. When in doubt we have adopted signs preferred by Gallaudet College.

Let us know how you find this book.

SHC
JLK
1991

Table of Contents

1

Numbers

1 | Numbers

Introduction

Word in the Hand, Book 2 is the continuation of *Word in the Hand*. It continues with the same format and style, building on the established vocabulary of *Word in the Hand*.

Word in the Hand, Book 2 will increase your signing vocabulary and strengthen your signing techniques.

Review

To begin, these *icebreakers* are a way for students to demonstrate their present level of signing facility and signing vocabulary. And in the social context, these icebreakers serve as a way for students to introduce themselves to others.

Choose one or combine several of the following icebreakers for each student to present.

1. My name is.....(finger spell).
2. How or why I learned to sign.
3. Tell something unique about yourself.
4. Have you had any occasion to use your sign language?

Students can speak as they sign and finger spell any needed vocabulary.

Introduce New Signs

This chapter is very long. It contains numbers as they are used in our many facets of communications. And, it contains vocabulary associated with numbers. Because of the length, this chapter may serve best as two lessons.

Numbers

The numbers presented here not only establish number signs but also how numbers are used in fractions, money, addresses, time, and ordination.

• Numbers 1 thru 29.

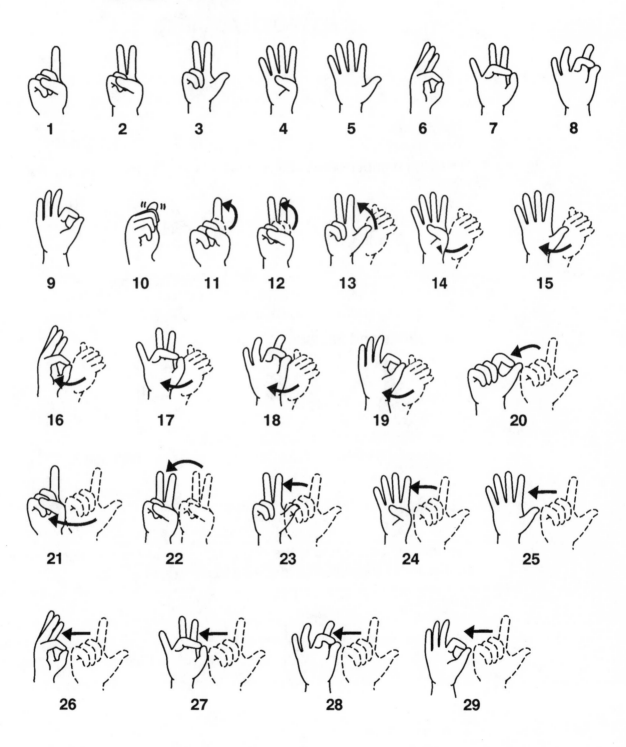

• Numbers 30 thru 99.

At this point, numbers become very consistant. Numbers become two separate digits, as in 34 and 60.

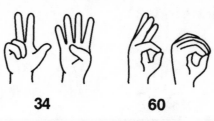

34   60

• Hundreds.

Break the number down. Sign hundreds first, followed by separate digits.

100   108

• Thousands and Millions

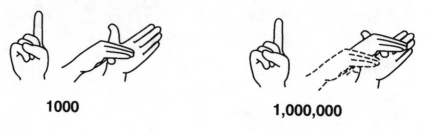

1000   1,000,000

• Fractions

The first number signed is the numerator. Move the hand down to sign the second number, which is the denominator.

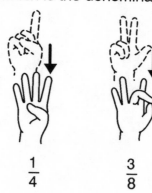

$\frac{1}{4}$ $\frac{3}{8}$

• Ordinal Numbers

Ordinal numbers are numbers like 1st, 2nd, 3rd, 4th, etc. Ordinal numbers under 10 use one sign. All other ordinal numbers use another.

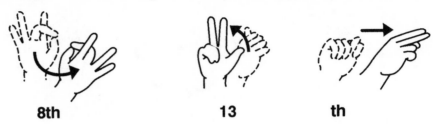

| 8th | 13 | th |

• Money

Money can be signed in two fashions. One, signs include dollars and cents. Two, signs only incude numbers. The context allows those conversing to understand the money connotation.

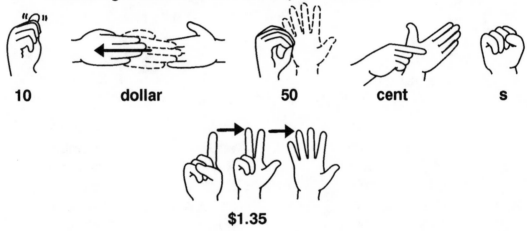

| 10 | dollar | 50 | cent | s |

$1.35

• Addresses

Break numbers down. Finger spelling is common for street names, including abbreviations like Rd., St., Av.

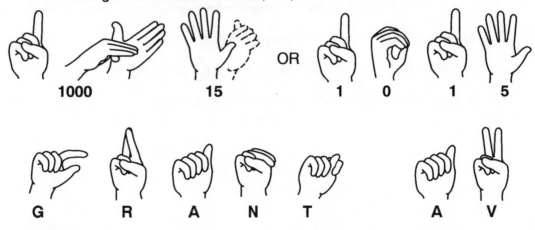

| 1000 | 15 | OR | 1 | 0 | 1 | 5 |

| G | R | A | N | T | A | V |

• Time

Two styles are presented. One, point to wrist to indicate time and sign the individual numbers. Two, point to wrist and sign the numbers over the wrist.

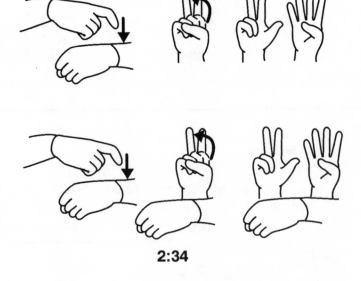

2:34

Vocabulary

add	dollar	multiply
address	equal	nothing
begin	few	number
cent	finish	plus
cost	fraction	several
count	how	size
date	minus	subtract
divide	money	twice

Exercises

1. Go over numbers and vocabulary twice.

2. Students can practice in small groups, especially the numbers.

3. Sign number examples for students to interpret.

6

Sentences

1. My father will be 50 years old on December 12th.

2. Be finished with your work at 6:15 tonight.

3. 32,000 people attended the football game.

4. One-half of the people began working at 12 o'clock.

5. More than twice as many bought cars by June 1990.

6. Count to 100 by 10s.

7. Several people live at 146 First St.

8. Today is the 17th, and next Monday is the 24th.

9. What does $5.14 and $6.12 equal?

10. Add the numbers: 214, 1200, and 82.

11. Few people live to be 99.

12. How much is 120 minus 74?

13. My address is 1476 Oak St.

14. Add the numbers 12, 132, 1201, and 17.

15. How much money do you get next week?

Assignment Possibilities

1. Be able to sign sentences in Part 5.

2. Be able to sign these phrases:

The date today is...	The time is...	How many...
How much...	How old...	What comes next...
What time...	The date is...	

4. Be able to sign:

7	11	January 11, 1946	10th
10	349	February 28, 1842	2nd
8	662	December 25, 1960	$2.87
16	527	March 4, 1776	$25.00
19	1400	November 22, 1911	$37.50
24	2422	April 1, 1990	$\frac{5}{12}$
37	$.01	October 31, 1800	
45	$.10	September 9, 1999	$\frac{1}{2}$
50	$1.00	June 16, 1952	

Vocabulary

add

address

begin

cent

cost

count

date

divide

dollar

equal

few

finish

Vocabulary

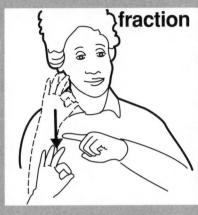 fraction

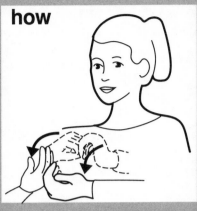 how

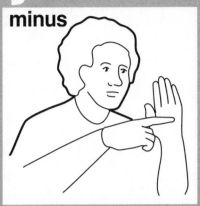 minus

 money

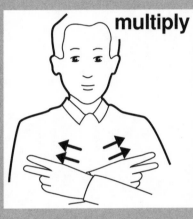 multiply

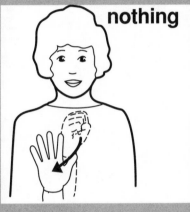 nothing

 number

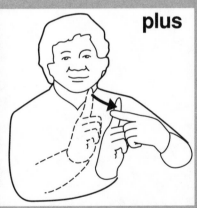 plus

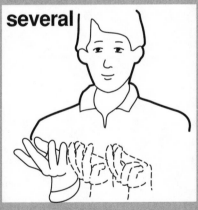 several

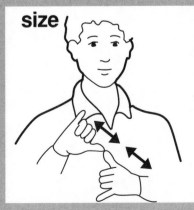 size

 subtract

 twice

2

Glue Words
& Modifers

2

Glue Words & Modifers

Signing Game

Sign All You Can

The leader designates a letter, for instance, *a*. The leader chooses an individual, randomly or in an order, to sign all words they can in 10 seconds (or set another time limit) that begin with the letter *a*.

To have everyone participate with the same letter, have everyone give one example until signs are exhausted.

This game can be expanded to include categories. Sign: colors; animals; clothing; food. Or, sign: things you would find at home or at school; things that are small and yellow.

Having the signer speak with their signed response reinforces the sign to all participants.

Review (All or Some)

1. Review signs from Lesson 1 vocabulary.

2. Review Sentences from Part 5, Lesson 1.

3. Review Homework Possibilities from Lesson 1.

Introduce New Signs

These words help to string language together. They are listed here in categories, but they often move between categories depending upon usage.

Special Note:

-er Sign Marker

To compare two of something: (1.) sign the comparing word; and, (2.) add this marker-

Vocabulary

Modifiers		Prepositions	Conjunctions
again	never	about	because
almost	often	above	either
away	only	across	or
best	soon	along	
better	sure	below	
each	than	beside	
enough	then	into	
ever	there	upon	
later	these	without	
less	those		
more	too		

Short words like *by* , *if* , *of* , *or* , and *so* are often finger spelled, it is quicker than signing.

Exercises

1. Go over the vocabulary twice.

2. Students can practice in small groups.

3. Sign words to students. Students tell what they are.

Sentences

1. Is seventeen more or less than twenty?

2. Only the best things are sold by Friday.

3. Put the ball away, and put it in there.

4. Do not run too fast.

5. I am sure she never walked across the street.

6. Either it is in the living room or it is in the kitchen.

7. I cannot go without my hat.

8. Find enough to carry home.

9. These are yours and those are mine.

10. It is later than you think.

11. Put these above the window and those below.

12. Sooner or later our cost will be twice as much.

13. Your sandwich is about as small as mine.

14. January is colder than June.

15. They went first, because they were next.

16. Have you ever been across the lake?

17. Bring it into the room, and put it beside the chair.

18. We must never forget.

19. One hundred twenty people can fit into the house.

20. He is funnier and better each time I see him on TV.

Assignment Possibilities

1. Be prepared to sign the Sentences in Part 5.

2. Be prepared to sign: My street address is...

    My telephone number is...

    Today is (day), (month) (number), (year).

    Start with 4, sign by 3s to 52.

3. Be prepared to tell what similarity in signing these words have:

    a. is, am, are, be.

    b. we, us, our.

Vocabulary

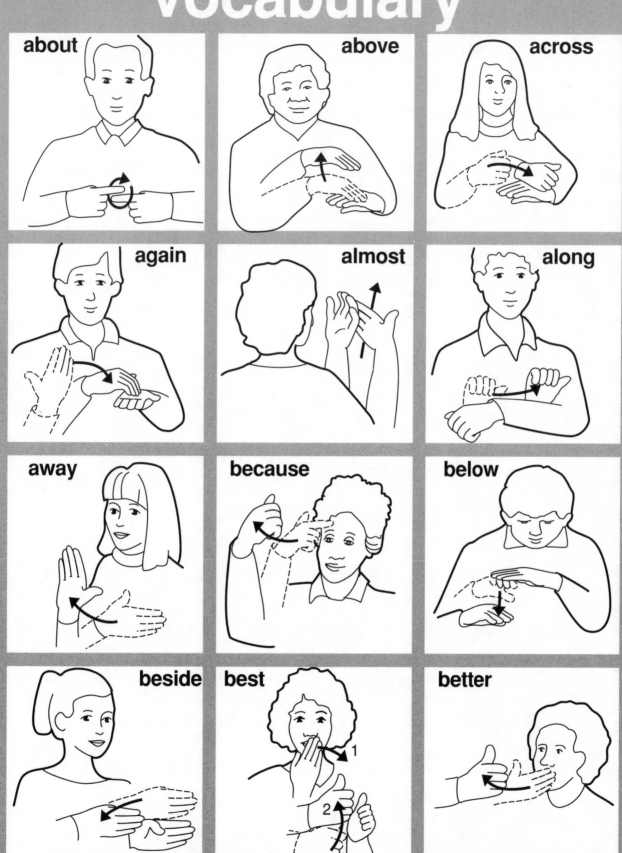

about

above

across

again

almost

along

away

because

below

beside

best

better

Vocabulary

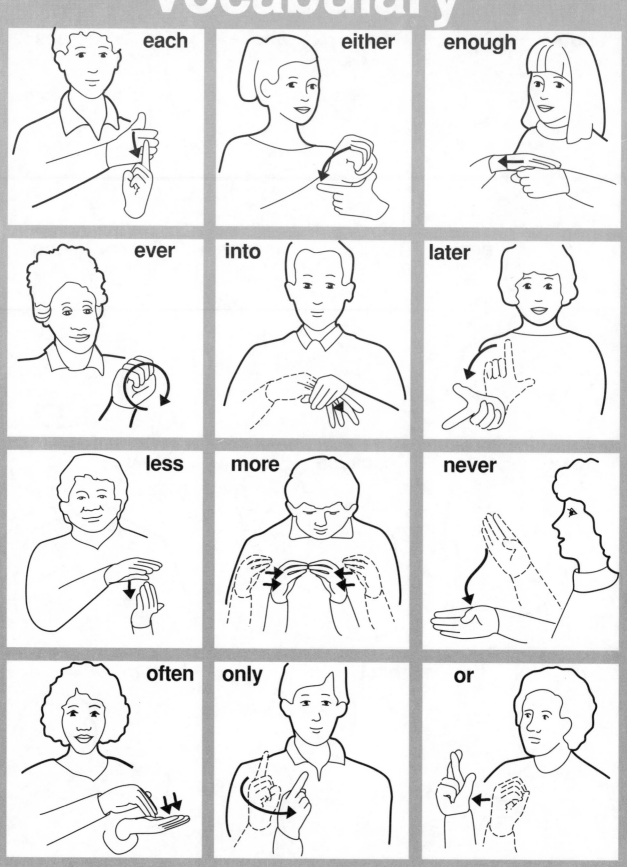

each

either

enough

ever

into

later

less

more

never

often

only

or

Vocabulary

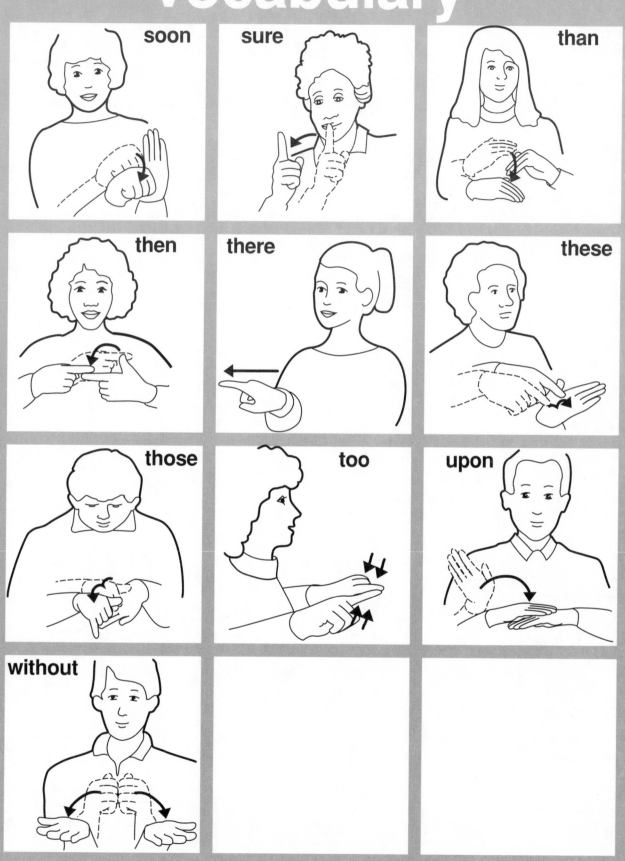

soon

sure

than

then

there

these

those

too

upon

without

3

Adjectives

3 Adjectives

Signing Game

What Comes Next?

A leader or volunteer signs 3 or 4 numbers that follow a consistant pattern—e.g., 3,5,7....

What come next? The person answering must provide the next number—e.g., "The next number is 9."

The leader can prepare a list or volunteers can make up their own examples spontaneously. Emphasize that patterns must be simple. Patterns that require paper and pencil or prolonged thought are not suitable.

Further examples: Subtraction   35, 25, 15.....
                     Division   200, 100, 50....
                     Addition   6, 11, 16....

Review (All or Some)

1. Review signs from Lesson 2 vocabulary.

2. Review Sentences from Part 5, Lesson 2.

3. Review Homework Possibilities from Lesson 2.

Introduce New Signs

Some adjectives were included in the last chapter. These adjectives are very common and simple adjectives. The -ly marker allows many of these adjectives to be used as adverbs. You have also learned about the -er marker used for comparisons. Another marker will be introduced for further comparisons.

Special Note:
-est Sign Marker
To compare two or more of something

Vocabulary

Adjectives

alone	easy	real
any	every	rough
awful	favorite	smooth
both	great	terrible
bright	kind	their
dangerous	most	usual
dear	other	wonderful
delicious	perfect	
difficult	proud	

Exercises

1. Go over the vocabulary twice.

2. Students can practice in small groups.

3. Sign words to students. Students tell what they are.

Sentences

1. Do you think the real address is 1410 Broadway?

2. Each person has their special place to put it.

3. Almost every size was too small.

4. The water made most streets dangerous to drive on.

5. They bought a great big doll without telling me.

6. Ice cream is delicious, but banana jelly is terrible.

7. The proudest person is my grandmother.

8. Is it smoother or rougher?

9. The brightest light is difficult to see.

10. Both puzzles are newer than yours.

11. He alone knows the best size.

12. Seventy-two is greater than 17 but smaller than 100.

13. They saw a great movie with their friends.

14. What an awful color!

15. She was very kind to buy several of my most favorite sweaters.

Assignment Possibilities

1. Be prepared to sign the sentences from Part 5.

2. Compose a simple 'What is...' riddle to be signed/finger spelled. State 2 or 3 qualities or characteristics as clues:

> What is green, grows in the ground, and has branches? (tree)

3. Be prepared to tell what similarity in signing these words have:

> a. they, then, their.

> b. breakfast, lunch, dinner.

Vocabulary

alone

any

awful

both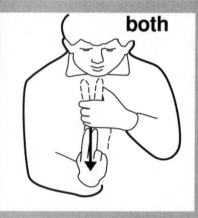

bright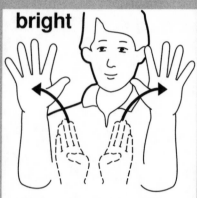

dangerous

dear

delicious

difficult

easy

every

favorite

Vocabulary

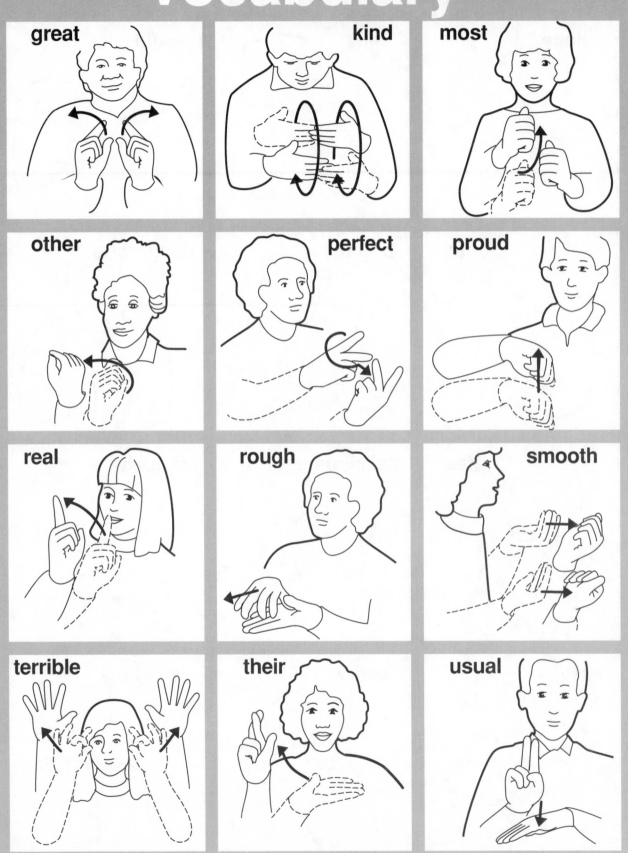

great

kind

most

other

perfect

proud

real

rough

smooth

terrible

their

usual

Vocabulary

wonderful

4

Verbs

4 Verbs

Signing Game

Compound Words

The leader or volunteer signs one part of a compound word. Others, randomly or in order, sign or finger spell what could be the missing part.

Examples:

rain/coat	**any**/one/body	**cow**/boy
snow/person/ball	**bed**/room	**lady**/bug
work/book	**house**/keeper	**sand**/box
every/where/thing	**fire**/person/house	**mouse**/trap
snow/ball/flake	**play**/ground/room	**bath**/tub/room

Can anyone think of compound words that are not two signs— such as motorcycle or butterfly?

Review (All or Some)

1. Review signs from Lesson 3 vocabulary.

2. Review Sentences from Part 5, Lesson 3.

3. Review Homework Possibilities from Lesson 3.

4. Review **comparative adjectives**: **-er** and **-est** markers; **more** and **most**.

Make these adjectives comparative:

easy	great	dangerous	bright
difficult	favorite	rough	delicious
large	afraid	ugly	hungry
cold	careful	new	clean
favorite	kind	alone	real
wonderful	awful	proud	special

Introduce New Signs

Special Note:

Pronouns: -body and -one.

anybody	anyone
everybody	everyone
nobody	no one

Sign *any*, *every*, or *no* and the appropriate ending for *body* or *one*.

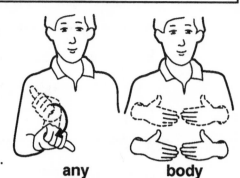

any   **body**

Vocabulary

You will notice that many of these new verbs are **auxilary** verbs.

become	hide	seem
believe	hold	shall
cause	laugh	should
change	let	spend
could	listen	tease
cry	might	wait
explain	owe	wish
fill	promise	would
frighten	recognize	worry
guess	save	understand

Exercises

1. Go over the vocabulary twice.

2. Students can practice in small groups.

3. Sign words to students. Students tell what they are.

Sentences

1. Do not worry.

2. The oldest man laughed at everyone.

3. You had better listen to what she wants.

4. Either come along with us or wait here.

5. Who do you believe might have changed the clock?

6. This is not a kind face, it frightens me.

7. Hide the bread, but save the butter.

8. The house seems awfully dirty.

9. I wish he would not bring anymore apples.

10. We should have enough money to spend.

11. Explain to everybody why you believe you are alone.

12. Do you recognize anyone across the street?

13. You owe us $12.50, plus several more boxes.

14. Stop teasing me!

15. Let those people hold the door.

16. Did you fill it with more than five or less than five?

17. They promised to meet us at 6:00 this evening.

18. I can guess almost every number.

19. Never begin without first thinking.

20. Count by 10s to 200.

Assignment Possibilities

1. Be prepared to sign the Sentences from Part 5.

2. Develop a short story or incident with at least four sentences.

3. Be prepared to tell what similarity in signing these words have:

      a. shirt, coat, blouse, sweater.

Vocabulary

become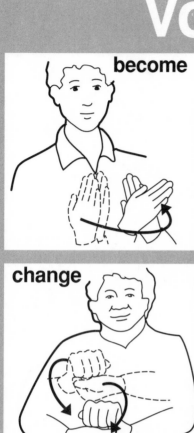

believe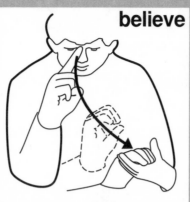

cause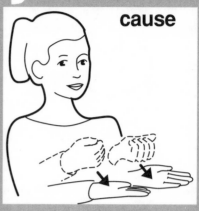

change

could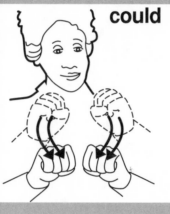

cry

explain

fill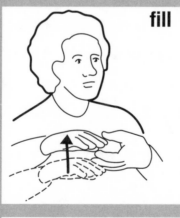

frighten

guess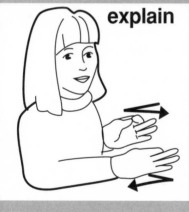

hide

hold

31

Vocabulary

laugh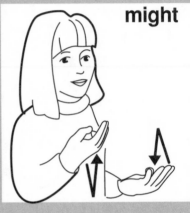

let

listen

might

owe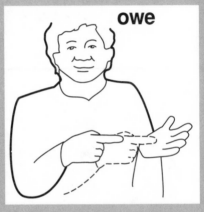

promise

recognize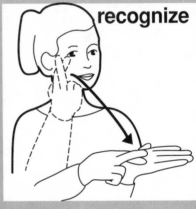

save

seem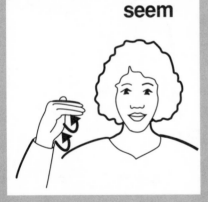

shall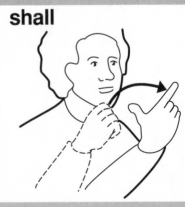

should

spend

Vocabulary

tease

understand

wait

wish

worry

would

5

Holidays & Special Occasions

5 Holidays & Special Occasions

Signing Game

Sign A Word

Leader has compiled a list of questions which are to be spoken. Answers must be signed. Answers can come randomly or in an order.

Questions should require thought.

"Sign a word..."

..with a silent e.
..that has a double consonant.
..that ends in (specific letter).
..that has 2 (3 or 4) syllables.
..that is an adjective (noun, verb) beginning with...
..that is an animal larger than....
..that is a green fruit.
..begins and ends with the same letter.

Review (All or Some)

1. Review the signs from Lesson 4 vocabulary.

2. Review Sentences from Part 5 , Lesson 4.

3. Review Homework Possibilities from Lesson 4.

Introduce New Signs

Special Note:
-'s Sign Marker
To make nouns possessive, add this marker:

Vocabulary

Holidays and Special Occasions

basket	Easter	Passover
birthday	eve	present
blow	game	pumpkin
bunny	ghost	receive
cake	Hanukkah	Santa Claus
card	holiday	Thanksgiving
carve	Halloween	Valentine
celebrate	merry	witch
Christmas	New Year	wrap
costume	parade	
decorate	party	

Exercises

1. Go over vocabulary twice.

2. Students can practice in small groups.

3. Sign words to students. Students tell what they are.

Sentences

1. My birthday comes after Hanukkah on January 11th.

2. The Halloween party sure was perfect.

3. People were dressed as ghosts and witches.

4. Which was your favorite present?

5. They sent Christmas cards to their best friends.

6. I might watch the Easter parade on television.

7. Who wants more cake?

8. Do you celebrate Christmas or Hanukkah?

9. That person carved the best pumpkin.

10. Did you have turkey, potatoes, and peas for Thanksgiving dinner?

11. Her 15th birthday was an occasion to celebrate.

12. I received your beautiful Valentine card.

13. It was not easy to wrap the Easter basket.

14. Her costume was not the usual Halloween ghost.

15. December 25th and January 1st are both wonderful holidays for our family.

Assignment Possibilities

1. Be prepared to sign the Sentences in Part 5.

2. Which holiday do you enjoy? Sign at least 3 sentences telling why.

Vocabulary

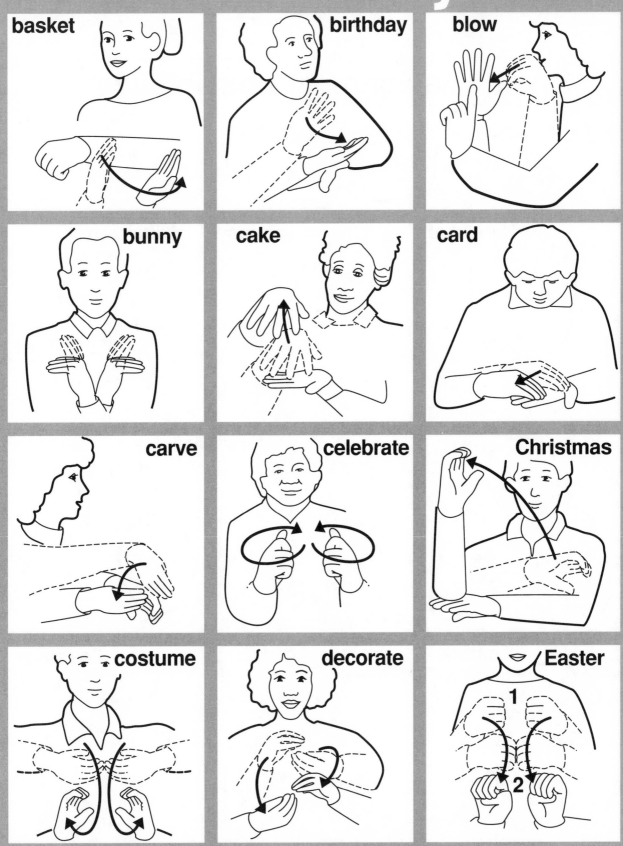

basket

birthday

blow

bunny

cake

card

carve

celebrate

Christmas

costume

decorate

Easter

39

Vocabulary

eve

 **game**

ghost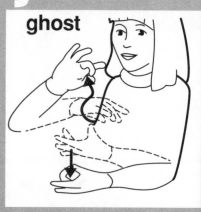

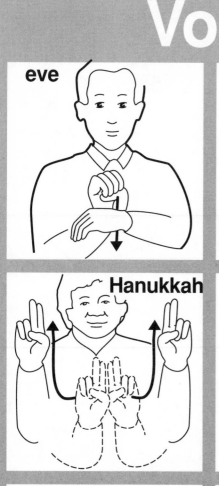 **Hanukkah**

 **holiday**

Halloween

merry

New Year

parade

 **party**

 **Passover**

Vocabulary

present

pumpkin

receive

Santa Claus

Thanksgiving

Valentine

witch

wrap

6

Neighborhood

6 Neighborhood

Signing Game

I Received

Leader begins by signing or speaking, "For Christmas/Hanukkah, I received." The leader adds what they received. Subsequent signers repeat all that has come before them, adding their present. The leader should encourage as much description as possible to make responses vivid: six yellow shoes; an elephant costume; a basket of spiders.

The listings can include all participants or begin anew after 5 or 6 presents.

Review (All or Some)

1. Review signs from Lesson 5 vocabulary.

2. Review Sentences from Part 5, Lesson 5.

3. Review Homework Possibilities from Lesson 5.

Introduce New Signs

The next three chapters expand from local to international surroundings, from the closeness of home to the distance of the world around us.

Neighborhood

apartment	gas station	temple
bank	job	town
beach	library	traffic
business	museum	vacation
camp	neighbor	zoo
church	picnic	
circus	pool	
city	restaurant	

Verbs

allow	begin	pay
answer	leave	remember
ask	order	try

Exercises

1. Go over vocabulary twice.

2. Students can practice in small groups.

3. Sign words to students. Students tell what they are.

Sentences

1. Do you know your nearest neighbor?

2. My mother's business is across the street from the bank.

3. Leave us at the museum, and we will ride the bus home.

4. We will have to pay $3 to get into the zoo.

5. There are four wonderful restaurants near our apartment.

6. Remember, the circus will be in town later this month.

7. My summer job is working at the library.

8. You should ask where the temple is.

9. The other job my brother has is answering telephones.

10. Our family's vacation will take us to the beach and the mountains.

11. How easy was it to travel through traffic?

12. Father spent $37 at each grocery store.

13. Did you walk the usual way to the swimming pool?

14. Our city is smaller than most but bigger than some.

15. Begin walking at 6 o'clock and camp by 8:30.

16. Try to remember the date of the picnic.

17. They listened but forgot about the parade.

18. Bring the other presents home on Christmas Eve.

19. Decorate the tree before December 12th.

20. Nobody seemed worried.

Assignment Possibilities

1. Be prepared to sign the Sentences in Part 5.

2. In at least three sentences, describe the neighborhood in which you live.

3. You have learned the word *family* in Book 1. It uses the letter *f* in co-ordination with hand movements. The words *group*, *class*, and *team* can be signed by letter substitution, while maintaining the same hand movements. Be prepared to sign: *group*, *class*, and *team* .

Vocabulary

allow

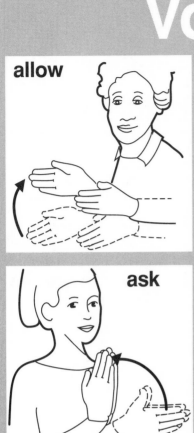

answer

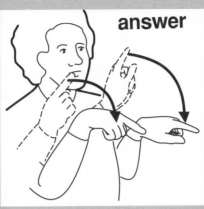

apartment

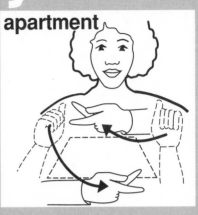

ask

bank

beach

begin

business

camp

church

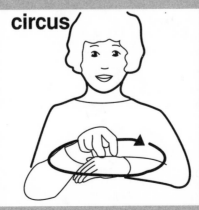

circus

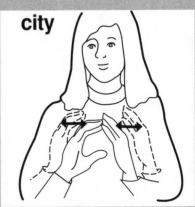

city

47

Vocabulary

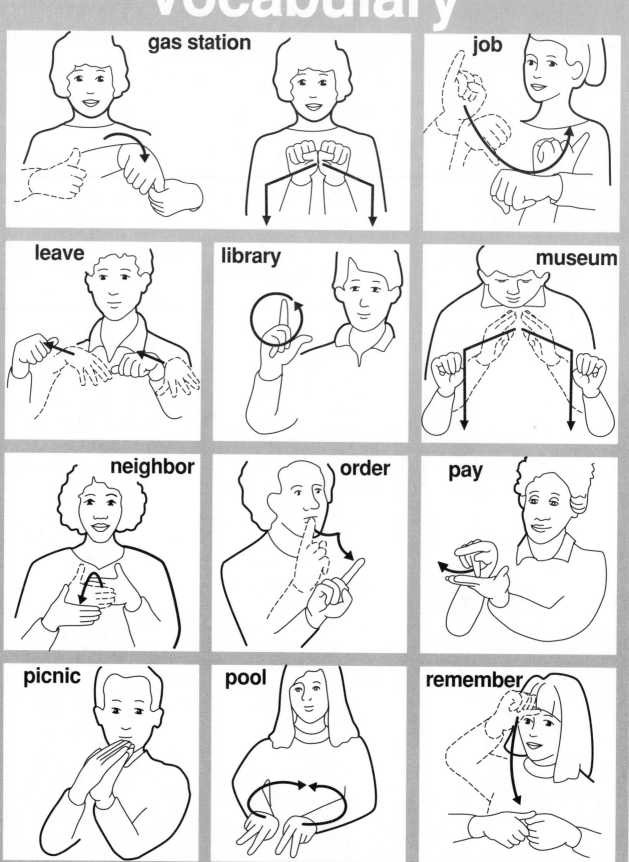

gas station

job

leave

library

museum

neighbor

order

pay

picnic

pool

remember

Vocabulary

restaurant

temple

town

traffic

try

vacation

zoo

7

Countryside

7 Countryside

Signing Game

What is...

Leader prepares a list of questions to be signed. For example:

What is...
an apartment	an ocean
a bank	a table
a business	a costume
a party	a basket
money	a holiday
a mountain	a zoo

Answers to these questions must be signed (within reason) to give at least two descriptions or definitions: "An apartment is a <u>tall building</u> <u>in the city</u> <u>where people live</u>."

Answers can be volunteered or an answering order can be established. But, answers must be made in complete thoughts, using as much signing vocabulary as possible.

Review (All or Some)

1. Review signs from Lesson 6 vocabulary.

2. Review Sentences from Part 5, Lesson 6.

3. Review Homework Possibilities from Lesson 6.

Introduce New Signs

Special Note:
Word Substitution

Signers must always be selective in their choice of words. This is especially true for synonyms and idiomatic expressions.

If a signer does not know a particular sign, a substitute can be used: a sign with synonymous meaning. Thus, similar adjectives like *big* , *large* , and *tremendous* might substitute for each other owing to context.

A more diffucult substitution process occurs with idioms. Idioms are words or expressions that are pecular unto themselves. For instance:

The horse <u>drew</u> the cart.	*Drew* means *pulled* .
Who will <u>run</u> for president?	*Run* means *compete* .
...head of state...	*Head* means *top* .
...butter fingers...	Unable to hold.

Literal signing of all words will not give the complete meaning of a signer's thoughts. A signer must substitute words to convey standard English meanings.

Vocabulary

Countryside

			Verbs
bridge	ground	ranch	cost
cattle	hay	rock	freeze
country	highway	seed	operate
earthquake	hill	storm	plant
environment	hurricane	thunder	plow
farm	land	tornado	
field	lightning	tractor	
garden	lumber	weed	

Exercises

1. Go over vocabulary twice.

2. Students can practice in small groups.

3. Sign words to students. Students tell what they are.

Sentences

1. The farmer plowed her land.

2. Operating a ranch is costly.

3. Every spring we pull weeds in our garden.

4. The tractor is across the field along with the truck.

5. Be sure to change your shoes before climbing the hill.

6. We have several thunder and lightning storms every summer.

7. The farmers around here plow in April and plant in May.

8. Highway 30 runs through our town.

9. The warmer the environment, the quicker the seeds will grow.

10. The earthquake frightened everybody in the neighborhood.

11. Go over the bridge and stop beside the lake.

12. My father plants seeds each spring.

13. We will use lumber from the mountains.

14. Our town has several churches, a grocery store, a bank, and many businesses.

15. The sheep dog moved the cattle into the plowed field.

Assignment Possibilities

1. Be prepared to sign the Sentences in Part 5.

2. Use at least three sentences to describe a short trip -real or imaginary- through the countryside.

3. Think of several word substitutions you might use for hard to sign or understand words and phrases.

Vocabulary

 bridge

 cattle

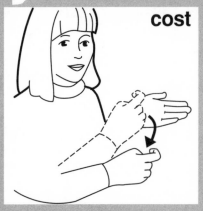 cost

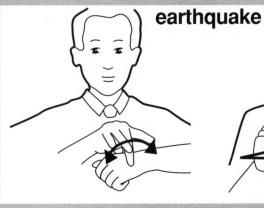 earthquake

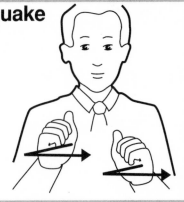

 environment

farm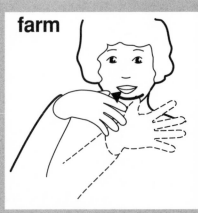

field

freeze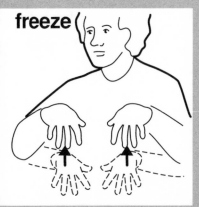

garden

ground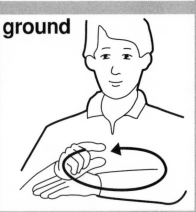

hay

Vocabulary

highway

hill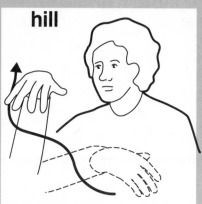

hurricane

land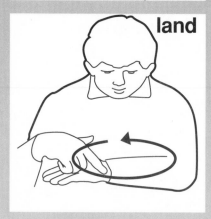

lightning

lumber

operate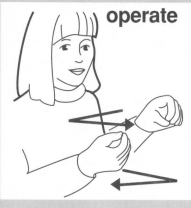

plant

plow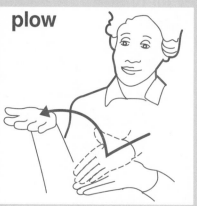

ranch

rock

seed

Vocabulary

storm

thunder

tornado

tractor

weed

8

Geography

8 Geography

Signing Game

Choose one.

Build a Story.

Leader signs one or several words as a story starter. In a random or established order, subsequent participants add words or phrases to build sentences and a story.

All preceding words should be signed before new words or phrases are added.

Leader should have several 'story starters' ready. Some stories will bloom, others won't.

Vocabulary Review

Leader states a category –colors, neighborhood, occupations, verbs, animals– and signs something from that catagory. Leader establishes an order of rotation.

Each participant signs something different belonging to the stated category.

Game should be paced. Participants must be attentive to past category examples, as examples can be used only once per game.

Review (All or Some)

1. Review signs from Lesson 7 vocabulary.

2. Review Sentences from Part 5, Lesson 7.

3. Review Homework Possibilities from Lesson 7.

4. Review Substitutions: How would you best convey these meanings?

> ...catch a bus..   ...run out of paper...
> ...pick up your feet...   ...all thumbs...

> The train <u>ran</u> between LA and SF.
> He <u>makes good</u> money.
> The game was a <u>draw</u>.
> She <u>did a take-off on</u> the farmer.
> The children had a <u>falling apart</u>.

Introduce New Signs

Special Notes:

Name Signs for Nations, Provinces, States, and Cities.

This third chapter dealing with the world around us has a focus not only on geographic features but also nationalities, provinces, states, and cities.

National, state, provincial, and local signs become less formalized and more regionalized as we move from nations to states and finally to cities. Standard signs are established for most nations, less established for provinces and states, and even less established for cities. This doesn't mean that small provinces, states, or cities don't have name signs. If they do, those signs are often particular to the area, holding less recognition the further one travels from that particular area.

Listing all possible signs for states and major cities would be an undertaking here —and perhaps too presumptuous. Local or regional adaptions would too often conflict to try and establish an explicit international sign for, say, Bismarck, North Dakota. But we must talk about states, provinces, and cities through our signing. Our compromise is to use abbreviations for states similar to the abbreviations used by mail services. For instance: Oregon–OR; Ontario–ONT; Nebraska–NE. This is one way to generalize for signing. If these abbreviations are not understood, finger spelling should be used.

Cities are another problem. Most cities will need to be finger spelled. Exceptions to this rule might be cities like: Los Angeles–LA and San Francisco–SF.

Formal signs are presented below for 13 nations. Suppose, for example, you know the sign for Canada, but you want to sign Canadian. Sign the nation, followed by the sign for person: country + person = a nationality.

Sharing signs that exist for cities, states, and provinces is interesting. Perhaps you know some.

Features:		river	**Verbs:**
capitol	east	state	arrive
coast	geography	south	born
desert	island	trip	return
direction	nation	valley	travel
earth		north	west

Countries:		Mexico
Africa	France	Russia
Australia	Germany	Scotland
Canada	India	Sweden
England	Ireland	UnitedStates/America

Exercises

1. Go over vocabulary twice.

2. Students can practice in small groups.

3. Sign words to students. Students tell what they are.

Sentences

1. I always enjoyed geography in school.

2. Where is the capitol building in Canada?

3. We traveled to England, France, Germany, and Russia on our vacation.

4. She was born on the west coast of Africa.

5. They left at 10:30 A.M. , and we arrived at 1:00 P.M.

6. Is California a state or a nation?

7. It was a terribly hot trip through the desert.

8. My mother and father were awfully happy to arrive here.

9. Their train ride took five days from the east coast to the west coast.

10. It was smoother than they thought it would be.

11. New York City is an island.

12. The earth seemed smaller than I had remembered.

13. They returned to their home in India.

14. Is there a best sign for Los Angeles or Chicago?

15. From which direction does the wind blow the hardest?

Assignment Possibilities

1. Be prepared to sign the Sentences from Part 5.

2. Create one or several signs that will creatively, though tastefully, depict a certain city, state, or nation.

Vocabulary

Africa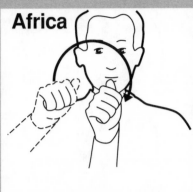

America

arrive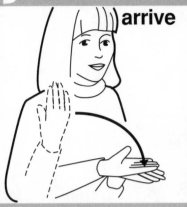

Australia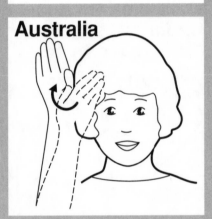

born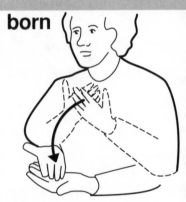

Canada

capitol

coast

desert

direction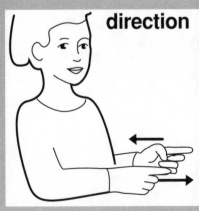

earth

east

63

Vocabulary

England

France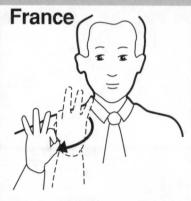

geography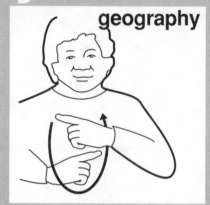

Germany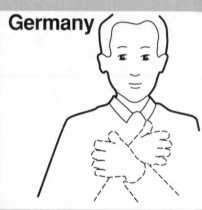

India

Ireland

island

Mexico

nation

north

return

64

Vocabulary

river	Russia	Scotland
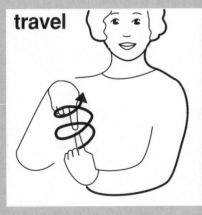		

river   Russia  Scotland

south 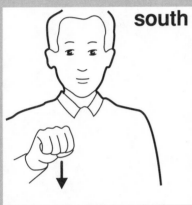 state  Sweden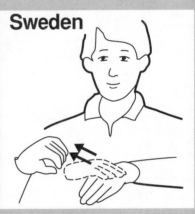

travel 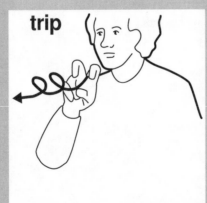 trip 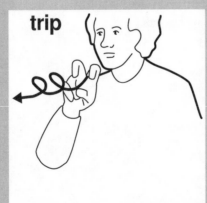 United States

valley 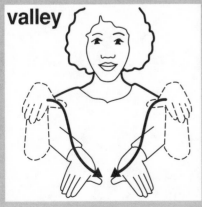 west

9

Medicine & Health

9 Medicine & Health

Signing Game

Choose one.

Countries

Leader signs a country. Those who will respond will describe something about that country.

Emphasis is to be on signing complete thoughts. The leader wants to elicit as many descriptions as possible, no matter how trivial, before going on to another country.

Those who sign can sign about such things as: climate, population, cultural habits, foods.

Addresses

Leader must prepare several addresses to be signed for interpretation. Be innovative with nations or states. A simple example might be:

> 12 1/2 Highway 30
> Los Angeles, CA 90607

The leader can break the address up, having the street address interpreted by one person and the city, state (nation, province) interpreted by another.

To extend the exercise, take several minutes and ask everyone to create an address —encourage creative addresses. Volunteers can sign their addresses for interpretaton.

Review (All or Some)

1. Review signs from Lesson 8 vocabulary.

2. Review Sentences from Part 5, Lesson 8.

3. Review Homework Possibilities from Lesson 8.

Introduce New Signs

accident	health	**Verbs**
ache/pain	medicine	breathe
all right	nervous	complete
ambulance	operation	cough
cut	patient	embarrass
disease	pill	happen
dizzy	poison	hurt
earache	shot	infect
examination	stomachache	vomit
fever	upset	
handicap	well	
headache	worse	

Exercises

1. Go over vocabulary twice.

2. Students can practice in small groups.

3. Sign words to students. Students tell what they are.

Sentences

1. I feel dizzy, and I have a stomachache.

2. Do you feel better or worse today?

3. The doctor should give her some pills for the fever.

4. What happened? You look nervous.

5. His stomach was upset.

6. The doctor gave me an examination after the accident.

7. Do not infect others with your cough.

8. My health could be better.

9. What kind of ache (pain) do you have?

10. You will be well in several days.

11. Someone call an ambulance quickly.

12. You will be all right after the operation.

13. This is the second shot he has received.

14. Do not drink that. It may be poison.

15. The examinaton was completed by 7:30.

 # Assignment Possibilities

1. Be prepared to sign the Sentences in Part 5.

2. You are going to a doctor with an illness —real or imaginary— or injury. Describe the symptoms and how the illness came about.

3. What is similar about signs for: *hospital*, *ambulance*, and *patient*? What is different?

Vocabulary

accident

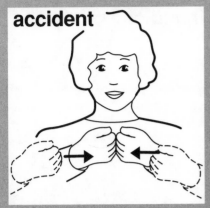

ache/pain

all right

ambulance

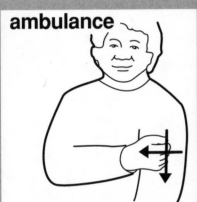

breathe

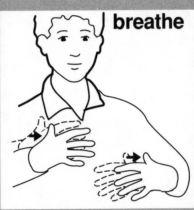

complete

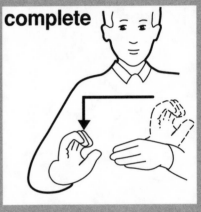

cough

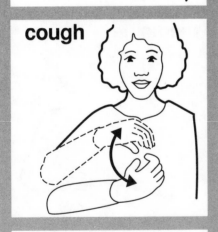

cut

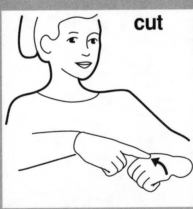

disease

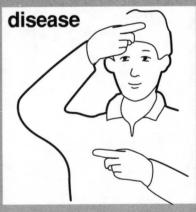

dizzy

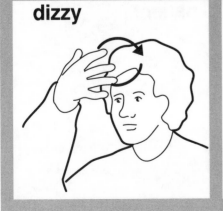

earache

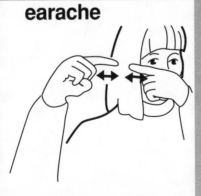

embarrass

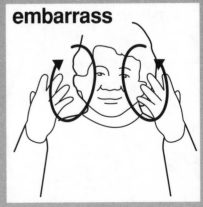

Vocabulary

examination

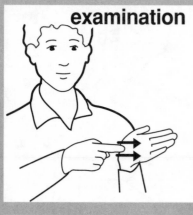

fever

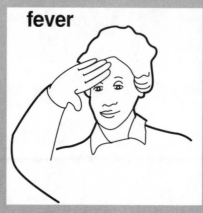

handicap

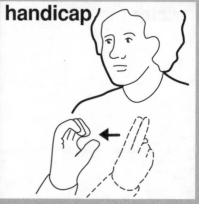

happen

headache

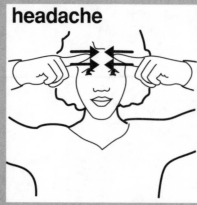

health

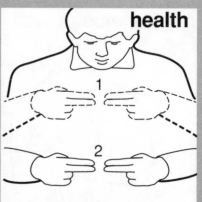

hurt

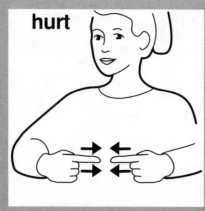

infect

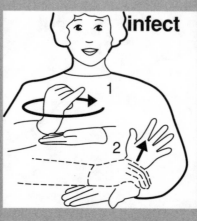

medicine

nervous

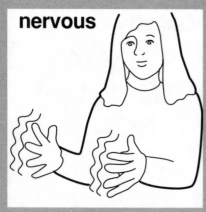

operation

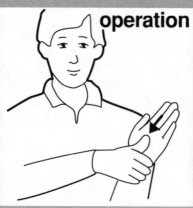

patient

Vocabulary

pill

poison

shot

stomach ache

upset

vomit

well

worse

10

Food

10 Food

Signing Game

Choose one.

Finger Spelling.

The leader signs, "I am thinking of a word that rhymes with_____". A word is finger spelled. Spelled words should be from a stated lesson. Vocabulary from a prior lesson can be reinforced in this manner.

rhyme

Examples, using Lesson 9:
I am thinking of a word that rhymes with <u>wealth</u> .   (health)
I am thinking of a word that rhymes with <u>cooperation</u>. (operation)

                              ...expect....   (infect)
                              ...purse...   (worse)

The person answering signs, "The word is _____" and signs their guess.

What Word?

Leader gives each participant a vocabulary word. Each person must create a sentence using that word. They must be able to sign the sentence omitting the word. Others must guess the omitted word.

The leader can also place the lesson from which the word came on the paper with the vocabulary word. The signer can, at some point, state the lesson as a clue to the word.

Review (All or Some)

1. Review signs from Lesson 9 vocabulary.

2. Review Sentences from Part 5, Lesson 9.

3. Review Homework Possibilities from Lesson 9.

Introduce New Signs

Foods

		Other
berry	pepper	better
carrot	pineapple	piece
cereal	pizza	sour
cherry	prune	sweet
corn	rice	taste
dessert	salad	
lemon	salt	
melon	snack	
noodle	spinach	
nut	tomato	
onion	vegetable	
peach	yoghurt	

Exercises

1. Go over vocabulary twice.

2. Students can practice in small groups.

3. Sign words to students. Students tell what they are.

Sentences

1. A peach is a fruit, not a vegetable.

2. I like blueberries, nuts, and cherries on my yoghurt.

3. Which is sweeter, the orange or the lemon?

4. Your breakfast cereal is beside the salt and pepper.

5. Let us change our breakfast time by one hour.

6. How awful. You put salt on your piece of pineapple.

7. Carrots are a favorite snack of mine.

8. Believe me. The milk is sour.

9. Taste this before you say anything.

10. We always buy sweet corn in the fall.

11. We should have a spinach salad, noodles, and dessert.

12. My brother who is a farmer grows many fruits and vegetables.

13. This year he planted tomatoes, onions, and melons.

14. We have a small garden, but we plant many of the same things each year.

15. No tomatoes on my pizza, thank you.

Assignment Possibilities

1. Be prepared to sign Sentences from Part 5.

2. Create a meal for someone —real or ficticious. Describe the offering.

3. *Noodle* is signed using hand motions while signing the letter *n* . *Macaroni*, *lasagna*, and *spaghetti* use the same hand motions but change the initial letter. Be prepared to sign macaroni, lasagna, and spaghetti.

Vocabulary

berry

better

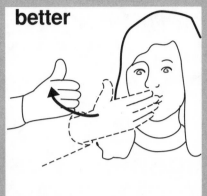

carrot

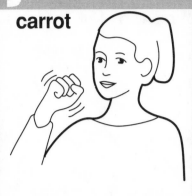

cereal

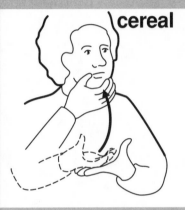

cherry

corn

dessert

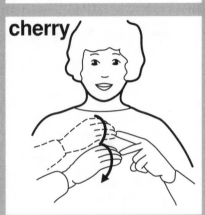

lemon

melon

noodle

nut

onion

Vocabulary

peach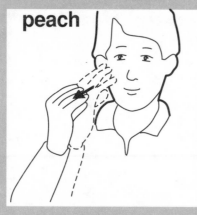

pepper

piece

pineapple

pizza

prune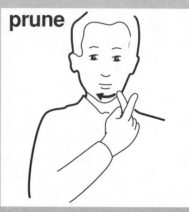

rice

salad

salt

snack

sour

spinach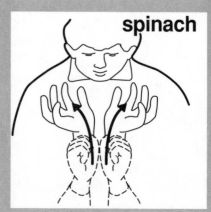

Vocabulary

sweet

taste

tomato

vegetable

yoghurt

Index

GARLIC·PRESS / MATH SERIES

Straight Forward Math Series

Addition #GP-006
Subtraction #GP-012
Multiplication #GP-007
Division #GP-013

The *Straight Forward Math Series* emphasizes mastery of basic math facts – addition, multiplication, subtraction, division.

Each workbook is a simple, straightforward approach to learning a specific mathematical operation. Each workbook is systematic, first diagnosing skill levels, then practice, periodic review, and testing.

Advanced Straight Forward Math Series

Adv. Addition #GP-015
Adv. Subtraction #GP-016
Adv. Multiplication #GP-017
Adv. Division #GP-018
Decimals #GP-020
Fractions #GP-021
Pre-Algebra Book 1 #GP-028
Pre-Algebra Book 2 #GP-029
Pre-Geometry Book 1 #GP-030
Pre-Geometry Book 2 #GP-031

The *Advanced Straight Forward Math Series* picks up where the earlier *Straignt Forward Math Series* ends.

SIGN LANGUAGE / HEARING GARLIC·PRESS

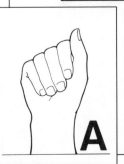

SOUND HEARING
#GP-026
SOUND HEARING provides listening examples to illustrate sound, hearing, and hearing loss. Listeners will hear as impaired people might, listening to music, a story, and taking a simple spelling test. All examples illustrate how hearing can be affected by variables of sound frequency and loudness.

An accompanying booklet provides the script of the audio tape.

A WORD IN THE HAND
#GP-008
A WORD IN THE HAND is a simple, basic primer to Signed English. It contains 15 lessons and nearly 500 illustrations. Each lesson provides vocabulary, illustrations, review, exercises, and assignments that students and adults will find exciting.

SIGN VOCABULARY CARDS
Set A #GP-023, Set B #GP-024
SIGN VOCABULARY CARDS teach simple, basic vocabulary and associated signs. Words have been chosen from basic sight and beginning vocabulary lists to combine with beginning sign language to aid signers in mastering first words and signs.

Two boxed sets, Set A and Set B. 100 words/signs per box. Signed English.

FINGER ALPHABET CARDS
#GP-009
FINGER ALPHABET CARDS are twenty-six sturdy 8 1/2" x 11" cards illustrating the finger alphabet.

These large cards provide the basis for all signing. They provide the beginning signer with the immediate reinforcement that spurs facility in signing.

SIGN NUMBER CARDS
#GP-022
SIGN NUMBER CARDS are 20 sturdy 8 1/2" x 11" cards illustrating numbers 1 to 20.

A complement to *FINGER ALPHABET CARDS*, *SIGN NUMBER CARDS* provide beginning signers immediate reinforcement.

GARLIC✿PRESS ENGLISH SERIES

Straight Forward English Series

Capitalization and Punctuation #GP-032
Nouns and Pronouns #GP-033
Verbs #GP-034
Adjectives & Adverbs #GP-035

The *Straight Forward English Series* is designed to measure, teach, review, and master specific English skills: *Capitalization and Punctuation; Nouns and Pronouns; Verbs;* and, *Adjectives and Adverbs.*

Each workbook is a simple straightforward approach to learning English skills. Skills are keyed to major school textbook adoptions.

Pages are reproducible.

SUBSTITUTE TEACHING GARLIC✿PRESS

Substitute Teacher Folder
#GP-027

Substitute Teacher Folders are pertinent information folders that regular classroom teachers fill out and leave for Substititue Teachers. The folder lists information such as class schedules, classroom procedures, discipline, support personnel, and regular classroom teacher expectations.

Substitute Ingredients
#GP-001

Substitute Ingredients is an informative collection of imaginative language arts, math, and art activities for grades 3 through 8. Reproducible master sheets accompany most activities.

Mastering the Art of Substitute Teaching
#GP-002

Mastering the Art of Substitute Teaching contains many practical ideas for teaching as well as ways to organize activities most effectively. The teaching formats, strategies, and activities are strictly from practical experience.

Classroom Management for Substitute Teachers
#GP-003

Classroom Management for Substitute Teachers discusses the substitute teaching role, suggesting procedures for *being-in-charge* in the classroom, establishing rapport, and getting the support of regular classroom teachers and staff.

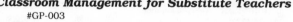
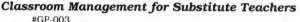

Lesson Plans for Substitute Teachers
#GP-014

Lesson Plans for a Substitute Teacher is a packet of 15 lesson plan forms. Each form can be easily filled out by regular classroom teachers to provide one day of instruction during their absence.